# My Side Of the Street

poems

## Martha Deborah Hall

Plain View Press
P. O. 42255
Austin, TX 78704

plainviewpress.net
sb@plainviewpress.net
512-441-2452

Copyright Martha Deborah Hall 2009. All rights reserved.
ISBN: 978-1-935514-26-8
Library of Congress Number: 2009931505

Cover art: *Amherst Church in Winter*, acrylic, January, 2006
by Michal Grace Everett.
Cover design by Susan Bright.

## Acknowledgements

Acknowledgments are due to editors of the following publications in which some of the poems in this collection appear:
SHEMOM, Abandoned Gardens and Poems from the Cranberry Room: "Left a Broken Heart"; Riversedge and The Poet's Touchstone: "melted snowmen"; Snap Poetry Journal: "Blue-Winged Chicken" and "Tears"; Abandoned Gardens Chapbook: "A chord"; Red Hawk Review: "Popping Greenies"; Seldom Nocturne: "Back Road to 'Our Town'"; Eye and The Poet's Touchstone: "Shedding Pine Needles"; Abandoned Gardens: "In St. Thomas"; Poems from the Cranberry Room and Abandoned Gardens: "just divorced"; Eye, Abandoned Gardens, and Poems from the Cranberry Room: "Priority Mail"; Abandoned Gardens: "Go Pick Blueberries"; Tapestries: "To my Valentines".

*For my mother,*

*Marjorie Elizabeth Collins*

# Contents

## Section I

| | |
|---|---|
| Ibble Obble (Out) | 9 |
| Left a Broken Heart | 10 |
| melted snowmen | 11 |
| Blue-Winged Chicken | 12 |
| (A) Chord | 13 |
| Baby | 14 |
| Popping Greenies | 15 |
| Triptych | 16 |
| Favorite Sounds | 17 |
| With a White Rose In Its Mane | 18 |
| Dave | 19 |
| Fall Calm | 20 |
| Back Road To "Our Town" | 21 |
| The Toy Bin | 22 |
| Shedding Pine Needles | 23 |
| In St. Thomas | 24 |
| just divorced | 25 |
| Priority Mail | 26 |
| Hey You | 27 |
| Downsizing | 28 |

## Section II

| | |
|---|---|
| Elm Street In the A M | 31 |
| Last Sunday | 32 |
| go pick blueberries | 33 |
| Memory Notes | 34 |
| The Ocean Is... | 35 |
| Tears | 36 |
| What If | 37 |
| Another Year Ends | 38 |
| Against My Walls | 39 |

## Section III

| | |
|---|---|
| At The County Fair | 43 |
| Things I Did | 44 |
| Saturday Night Dance | 45 |
| River Running Through It | 46 |
| The Baby Grand | 47 |
| Crumbled Dreams | 48 |
| Big Girls Don't Cry | 49 |
| Why Go In Today? | 50 |
| Leftover Buzzing | 51 |
| The Last Time I Saw You | 52 |
| West Of the Ocean, South Of the Moon | 53 |
| This Year In Review | 54 |

## Section IV

| | |
|---|---|
| Deliverance | 58 |
| Girl With Kerchief | 59 |
| Loving Others More Than Ourselves | 60 |
| I'll Remind Myself Of | 61 |
| The Bottom Of the Well | 62 |
| As the Clock Runs Down We Can Still... | 63 |
| But I Do | 64 |
| Gloves | 65 |
| Tea Party | 66 |
| To My Valentines | 67 |
| Packing | 68 |
| Move Back To My Old Hometown | 69 |
| Close Contact | 70 |
| Notes Incarnate... | 71 |
| Runaway | 72 |
| Think Of Me... | 73 |
| sublime | 74 |
| Where the Grass Is Green | 75 |
| End Of Day | 76 |

About the Author     77

# Section I

# Ibble Obble (Out)

*Ibble obble black bobble*
*Ibble obble out*
*Turn a dirty dishcloth inside out*
*Once if it's dirty*
*Twice if it's clean*
*Ibble obble black bobble*
*You are out!*


At my purple playhouse with the Dutch door
mostly sad memories are what I recall.
As I search for the old key near the stone wall,
things surface that long ago had been shored:
my black cat Muggs eating mix off the floor,
how she toyed with a live mouse like a ball,
the limpid eyes of the hanging deer in the stall,
all the stained garden party dresses I wore.

Years filled with cracked tea cups, half-baked apples,
childhood bullies, snowballs turned to ice. I learned to count
on myself in life's scheme of things, tried to grapple
with sliced- in- two dreams, and yet they mounted
like a sink in which soiled, stacked dinner plates topple,
end up at our feet broken, bobbled, squandered, daunted.

## Left a Broken Heart

I don't own anything of mother's
except a glued plate once cracked in two.

There was a small sapphire ring.
Father buried it with her.

## melted snowmen

window ice frames my reflection
bending branches slap the roof
it's freezing in the front room
stone cold coffee in the pot
present wrapped in newspaper
sparse tinsel on a fake tree
shattered ornament on the floor
dripping umbrella in the hallway
bittersweet wreath on the door
a snowplow clangs its iron song
to me all snowflakes look the same

## Blue-Winged Chicken

A plane ticket
to San Juan with it,
whole milk for it as we fly.
Lift legs high as
doctor dilates
and scrapes,
flips the mirror,
dims the light.
Fly home without...
birth certificate.
Girl? or Boy?
No body,
No name.
No first words,
no steps,
no childhood, no grave.
Down, down.
Ground down I fly.
You're dead
so I can live.
No, I die, you live.
Red milk tonight
flows and streams
in a dark room, on
a floor, on a bed.
Red, red, into
night-days.
Auf wiedersehen,
Adjo, farewell~
Sorry, sorry.

# (A) Chord

Tinkling plaints of piano keys

filling the empty room

end on

reflective notes—

what could have been—

      what is—

           what will be—

                harmony

# Baby

Dressed in striations
of violet and yellow,
splashed in shades
of pink, rescued from the
crevice of split tar,
carried home,
cradled in a Starbucks
vanilla frappuccino bottle,
tap water nourished,
the lobelia lives on the white
kitchen counter beside
the stainless sink.

## Popping Greenies

sun's up
wind brisk
flags flap
cars packed
cooler full
on our way

there
we hoist sails
secure lines
starboard wind
blows off the bow

we dash start
sail glide through
the blue sea carpet

the isles of shoals
to our right
we glimpse
sea grass spikes in
celia's garden

we're first  we're first
across the finish line

we pop two
heinekens    toast

to the go fast boat
in the harbor

to the go fast boat
in the harbor

# Triptych

1.
Oilskins
on. Sails topside.
Turbulent seas ahead.
Stay on the boat, don't cut and run.
Bring to.


2.
Gangplanks
are gone. Anchor
line's free. Where should we go?
Fly like seagulls. Circle life's trip.
Don't yaw.


3.
Boom slams
back and forth. Boat's
adrift, currents pull. Wherever we two end up, that port
will do.

## Favorite Sounds

Your quiet breathing at two am, the rooster down the road crowing,
clink of a silver spoon against a Lenox teacup, church bells
Sundays at ten, wind-shield wipers in the rain, Piaf singing,
"non, je ne regrette rien," the cessation of the dentist's drill,
the crunch of snow as I walk, my neighbor mowing
his golden field, grandchildren splashing in the pool,
the humming air conditioner in ninety degrees,
ice cubes tumbling into glass, and, of course,
the doorbell buzzing that you're here.

## With a White Rose In Its Mane

The horse was white, the carriage too,
on our buggy ride through Central Park.
His harness white, our spark was new.
The horse was white, the carriage too.
Wheels were white, white leather shoes.
The Plaza white with springtime hues.
First the carriage was white, then blue
on our buggy ride through Central Park.

# Dave

So gentle
So soft-hard to anger
Darling bird on the sill
The buoy that clanged in each day
The night owl out on the maple
My pot of simmering goodness
My salt of the earth, my spade
Ski pole that dug in each day
My hammer, my saw, my daffodil
My hazelnut cup of coffee
Rooster with cute staccato crow
My couch potato when it rained

## Fall Calm

Half an acorn drops on my right sneaker.
Leaves—yellow, yellow, one green.

My son Carl is still at the dock,
fishing with his dad.

Where did Summer's storms go?

# Back Road To "Our Town"

Chopin and I are alone in the car
8 AM Saturday
mist clears
sunlight's alive
gas tank's full
no traffic
green acorns all over the ground
roadside stands of pumpkins ripe for pies
gold leaves dance on the windshield
breeze
red leaves checker lawns
a garden hose drips on a stone wall
next to me my maroon sweater
in the back seat, boat shoes and a life jacket
the canoe port is up ahead
Chopin and I cruise along in the car

# The Toy Bin

My children packed their boxes and went away.
Tin soldiers capture the abandoned rooms.
The xylophone on the porch refuses to play.

Their bicycles rest; spokes rust in the hay.
Pink chalk marks on the walk gone too soon.
Each child filled a trunk and went on his way.

The walls emptied of sketches have no say.
Raggedy Anne broods in her dollhouse tomb.
The xylophone on the porch refuses to play.

The spin has gone out of the top since that day
Helium escaped the red birthday balloons.
My children forged their memories and went away.

The Barney record croons no tune today
And dusty toy arrows no longer zoom.
The xylophone on the porch refuses to play.

A Chicken Little storm sweeps down in May.
Cinderella won't reclaim her old straw broom.
The children packed up and left, went far away.
The xylophone on the porch refuses to play.

## Shedding Pine Needles

Pink and cream buds from a Monet Twilight Poinsettia
fall on the tablecloth, obscure a child's hot chocolate stains.

In my neighbor's window, snuffed white candles.
Outside a plane flies south of the snow.

The once-crazed household is empty.
My lipstick's smeared from so-longs.

A Laura Ashley sock tag remains on the couch.
The Baby Gap box holds returns.

The evergreen tree needs watering.
The "Scrabble" game sits on a card table.

There's leftover turkey for supper,
a piece of pecan pie.

I want to hug each loved one once again.
A champagne bubble bursts inside.

# In St. Thomas

with our 55' yawl moored in the harbor,
we savored a gourmet supper on the pier—
escargot, Crab Rangoon and meringue.
Tipping the violinist for playing our song,
*Solitaire*—"the only game in town"—
*Solitaire*—the name of our former 30' sailboat,
you and I left as the music ebbed.

Low-tide waves lapped against the boat.
Topside, under a rainless sky, a void filled
me. I couldn't laugh, smile or speak a word—
went inward. The marriage had run aground.
I was alone in an ocean of uncoiling.
This 20-year voyage rested on my watch—
I was an anchor that couldn't hold.

## just divorced

one plate
i take
down
from
the
cup-
board

i sit
eat
a lone
l(one)
loner-
sole
emp
ti
ness
some
lone
li
ness
just
lone
ly
period
call
sis
to
comfort
me
hang up
take
out
the trash

# Priority Mail

An old wooden box in my attic holds
three postcards from the man I married.

One drawer of my favorite desk keeps
notes from my homesick children.

A steel cabinet guards
two copies of my will.

In a tin box, carefully hidden,
seventeen sensuous letters from you.

# Hey You

lawn sprinkler system s off    down quilt on the bed    swimming
pool closed    ski mobile ready      the ancient furnace puffs and
coughs      a crimson maple spills its bushels of maroon leaves
i nudge a pine cone in the driveway to rest on fallen needles    our
storm door in place      the screen in the barn    the supply of hay
replenished in the loft      the waterfall slows near the river bank
van cliburn plays rachmaninoff    i mend my woolen sweater its four
o clock  on saturday afternoon       i d call you if you were still alive

## Downsizing

At my new digs on Stark Street, I practically
live in my neighbor's pockets. I open my door and hear
children laughing across the way.

Politicians in red ties give speeches in the square and a
hometown band plays "Margie," my mother's name
as I meander home from a walk.

A weeping willow stands outside my window and there's
a duck crossing sign near the canal. My socks in the drawer
finally match and my penny loafers seem at home.

I give the photos of you to the kids.

# Section II

# Elm Street In the A M

Shelter doors open at seven.
Homeless pour into the street.
Some carry knapsacks~most nothing.
Others push carts filled with empty cans.
Stained coffee cups strewn on the sidewalk.
Cigarette butts everywhere.
I lower my eyes as I pass;
seal the lockbox inside myself.

Burnt toast permeates the air.
Town workers push dirt with Bobcats.
Inland seagulls fly from the dust.
One man dries socks on his dashboard.
A vet gets hit with a ticket.
A Segue speeds on my left.
Three motorized wheelchairs whiz by.
An ambulance is being towed.

The roof of St. Anne's Church has caved in.
Interfaith Tree Plantings are dead.
Moss grows along the granite curb.
There's a Beneficial Finance.
Two blocks away is a pawn shop.
The Youth Art Center's boarded up.
There's a dead pigeon on the ground.
Last week it was a small sparrow.

## Last Sunday

We turned clocks ahead an hour.
All the ice was gone from Red Moon River.
Mallards returned to Silver Pond.
Flags fluttered from porch rails.
Hank's Hot Dog Stand reopened.
The tennis club's courts were swept.
I slathered butter on whole wheat boule rolls.
My neighbor gassed herself.
She was dead anyway.

## go pick blueberries

for breakfast

        have some for

                      lunch

          you like them

                      for supper

I was glad when she died

# Memory Notes

marched in tune to the beat played on the fife and drums of her life
as she sat and gazed across the golden fields of autumn that night
that once had glided her to calming waltzes through winters of strife,
moved her to recall the varied melodies that had chaptered her life.
The polonaise slashed through her soul with its keen silver knife.
Being brave, she bowed to the fugue's crescendo finale in her flight.
Gone were the high-lows, non-stop dissonance resounded in her life,
as for the last time, she gazed across rain-soaked fields that night.

# The Ocean Is...

volcanic, vibrant, silent,
singing, strong-willed, vivacious,
temperate, tenacious, raucous,
racing, graceful, gracious,
scintillating, lovely, lonely,
perplexing, perpetual, unpredictable,
buoyant, beckoning, bewildering,
encompassing, infuriating, inspiring
giver of life which is why
we placed my sister's ashes in her body.

**Tears**

jumped from my chair
pulled on my eyelashes
bolted around the room
slapped my face twice
squeezed my eyes shut.
I blasted the CD player
to turn them off.

# What If

...elephants left home to join the circus,
...the robin whistled, the train whistle cooed,
...a tortoise entered and won the Boston Marathon
...death ever left the room

## Another Year Ends

Snowman,
a god from child-
hood, with carrot nose, coal
eyes, symbol of my early bliss,
melting.

## Against My Walls

The 5 AM "Canal"
screeches
over silver tracks.
Its mournful horn
prods me into
another morning.

My laptop wordsmith ticks,
sending seconds to the wind.
Upon wakening it orders
"Don't waste today."

"Tock"
shouts
the fiercely-
painted flower
standing at attention
against the glass-doored chest.

Its piercing orange and white
judge every night
how well
I've played with time.

# Section III

## At The County Fair

The day after a hard frost, I order a cup of
Green Mountain coffee and watch a gray-
bearded man with a chain dangling from
his dungarees. He stands in the shadow of
the concession stand in red-stained cow-
boy hat cocked to the left and black leather
boots with spurs. He spits a wad of chewing
tobacco; drools brown juice from his lips. He
leers at the girl with a white ribbon in her hair,
being led on a horse around the corral. When
finished, he helps her get off, placing his arm
below her waist. A freight train whistle blows.

## Things I Did

My arms outstretched toward the side of the bed where he used to sleep, I remember how he was the one who always lost the choose-up game to see who would fetch the morning's first cup of coffee, the one who delighted in the brilliant hues of September leaves, the one who led his life his way--ethically, morally, successfully, the one who loved how I made crème brûlée, the one who placed flowers on my parents' graves, the one who once brought me two goldfish in a crystal bowl because I said I was lonely during the day, the one who made me a cassette of the arias I loved in my youth, the one who left me because of me.

## Saturday Night Dance

Afternoon brightness blinks. Rain streams down
the street as wipers swipe windshields on passing
cars. Yet another Anna Nicole Smith TV snippet—
once her last name was Hart. I should start the
dishwasher but instead stare at fake sunflowers
in an aluminum watering can. The wall clock marks
empty seconds with loud clicks. I don't want supper.

## River Running Through It

Only one bite of yellow apple left as I sit
in my grey jeep looking out over the choppy,
inviting river.  A girl's green bicycle is chained
to the black iron guard rail. A dozen noisy
tourists clomp by, interrupt my peace of mind.

# The Baby Grand

I sat in the big chair. *It seemed big then.*
The metronome marked time, ticking, ticking.
She wore a summer dress, pink, blue and green,
sat on a stool with glass and ball footing.
I listened across the room in this scene.
The afternoon sun faded, started receding.
Rose petals danced to the floor, so serene.
All the downstairs continued darkening.
Piano notes float through the air now.
*I asked her once before. She said "Chopin."*
I wonder if she was able to know
what joy her music brought to my being.
She left the room without taking a bow,
picked up coral petals without seeing...

## Crumbled Dreams

Crows caw as I drive down Christian Hill Friday morning. A heavy breeze blows leaves off the crimson maple which stands next to the brown house with the chipping paint. Off to the left are remnants of a vegetable garden, slouching cornstalks. The lawn covered with broken branches; a blue shovel left in the sandbox. Missing seats, dangling ropes slap against metal braces of the swing set. A stuffed tiger lies face down. Window flower boxes bear weeds. Shades are drawn. A torn American flag flaps on the front porch next to where a basketball hoop has toppled. Broken ochre pots lie abandoned.

Four other people arrive and stand as a maroon jeep pulls into the driveway, parks next to the broken down granite wall. The Bank's auctioneer slams a sign in the ground: "Notice of Sale of Real Property—Foreclosure at 10 AM".

# Big Girls Don't Cry

We were some of the first to arrive and the last to leave. From cloth diapers to a navy blue tux, from a pitcher's glove to a gold wedding ring, from crooning of Willy's songs in the family car thirty years ago to "Panis Angelicus" sung from the balcony above the congregation at St. Cecelia's Church on Saturday afternoon. Pews were filled with wonderful friends and family, some of whom I may never see again.

*Now the dismal solitude* of my empty condominium at the lower end of Canal. May Day, but it is cold. Turned on the gas heat again. My mother-of-the-groom outfit is still in the suitcase in the backseat of my car, three days later. The orchid I held during the ceremony rests on a plate in my living room next to the white invitation. Why can't every day be as much fun as the wedding was? Why can't I get over this? No one can pull me out. I'm lost. No one can find me. Not even you.

## Why Go In Today?

I go back to bed at 9 A.M.
The "Today" show is over. <click>
Six chicks need a new pen on PBS. org for kids. <click>.
Ellen is wearing a new red necktie. <click>
Regis speaks of the passing of "Scooter" Phil Rizzuto. <click>
Kelley shows off a huge pimple on her neck. <click>
Imus is coming back on the air for $20 million. <click>
Channel 13 has a weight gain cure. <click>
<click>

# Leftover Buzzing

Orange lights on the Christmas tree and window
candles take small swipes at the dark. A honey-
colored wreathe swats the front door. Tomorrow it's back *to*
nectar from a tangerine. I flutter through two pages of
a yellow-jacketed book and then call my daughter on my *new*
flip phone. Shall I call my vespine upstairs neighbor
and wish him happy new year's tidings too? Has his venom
sunk in deep enough? Wait! Is that a sting I feel, whirring
wings I hear, descended from attic snowfields?

On the kitchen table, buds on holiday flowers close.

## The Last Time I Saw You

I can hardly write it...so jaundiced, so jaundiced. You looked like you had thrown it in without the fight...So tired, so barren of hope, with wig in place to disguise cancer's rage. So alone, so alone, with once outstretched hands now closed in tight fists. I try to understand the whys of it—this thing we once called life—the trotting, galloping, cantering of us, ponies in the open spring fields. The page before me fills, shadowed by the vision of that truth called death... life's solution, the final kiss before they shut the coffin, the clanging of the last bell, the last note in the aria, the tear that asks why did I bother, the one last glance before I bid adieu, the last spark that shoots against the brick before it bows to night, then darkened is the room, the icicle that slips into the nowhere, like the cricket smashed against the back door screen, the carrying off of a red leaf in the wind, the mud that forges to the drain, the darkened house at 1 AM, the book with the last match gone, the pair of cozy slippers thrown into the trash, the fountain pen that's out of ink, the apple pie that's been devoured, coffee without a cup, salt without the French fries, a cookie without a small hand reaching for it.

# West Of the Ocean, South Of the Moon

Gone carved initials in the maple tree.
Love's winding road did not wend our way.
Once wild, now tame, where does fulfillment flee.

Wherever I went, you were there with me.
High tides, then low, the high refused to stay.
Gone are carved initials in the maple tree.

No more speeding down Summer Hill on skis.
Pink cartons, stenciled high chairs now tossed away.
Once wild, now tame, love's embraces flee.

Splintered, the polished floors we waltzed on 'til 3.
Why refuse to accept what has had its say.
Gone carved initials in the maple tree.

No time machine, can't rewind this story.
Perdita, snowy ice drips on my face today.
Once wild, now tame, where does loyalty flee.

Latches on our hearts must have broken free.
All fantasy balloons have flown astray.
Gone carved initials in the maple tree.
Once wild, now tame, where does constancy flee.

## This Year In Review

**January**
Greenhouse effect winter: dogwoods bloom

**February**
Pay Christmas credit card bills

**March**
A fly

**April**
Swan boats on the common

**May**
Bring chrysanthemums to her grave

**June**
Grandkids on monkey bars

**July**
Steaks on the grill

**August**
Sail-sail-sail

**September**
Iced tea's last fling

**October**
Cobwebs

**November**
Turkeys everywhere

**December**
Mitten on the sidewalk

# Section IV

## haiku

waiting under the Elm
no break in the rain
or my loneliness

# Deliverance

Humpbacked is how I am, alone on
an island with my heart of wood. Out
of cloth diapers for decades, so
where's the promised warmth apart from the
embryo, the whispering grass that
asks me to join in? Where's the swimming
hole with nearby water lilies, the
white cake smothered with vanilla ice
cream? What happened to the Bible I
once believed in, the hope that one day
I'd feel I belonged? Is there a way
to deliver myself from evil?
How can I unring the bell, the bell?

# Girl With Kerchief

Seeing her at my Doctor's office,
hairless, clutching her capped urine sample,
made me stop and catch my breath.

## Loving Others More Than Ourselves

She worked as a nurse on the night shifts, came home and made us breakfast—usually fried eggs with bacon for Kappy, homemade deep-fried donuts in sizzling fat for me. As children she allowed us to sit in and talk during the 5 o'clock "adult hour," bought us red wooden pails for summer beach mornings, handmade us identical senior prom dresses with spaghetti straps, had a jeweler fashion sapphire rings for our September Sweet Sixteen, made a lace cap to go with my wedding dress, gave up her house for a week so Kappy and her husband could spend their honeymoon there. She was the first one through the door the day our mother died and she came to us to spend the first Christmas after it with us. I remember Kappy sitting in her lap in dad's black leather chair telling her how she missed "mommy." On summer vacations she'd lug a straw basket of sandwiches to the beach and we'd sit there, eat them on the blanket on the sand under the red beach umbrella. Or we'd run over to the local dairy in the early evening hours where she'd treat us to peppermint stick or maple nut ice cream cones. She taught us to be ourselves, to love ourselves, to comprise our messages in life not of words but of actions. She said to live in the now and not in the yesterdays or tomorrows, this Aunt, this Mildred Lee of our lives, our world.

## I'll Remind Myself Of

the blue robin's egg in the country, seagulls at the shore,
daffodils high on Meredith's winding hill
when at the cusp of dawn the river sliced the fields;
I'll see the log we crossed to reach the far side of the
brook to climb the hill and watch cows graze in golden fields;
I'll see the full moon at the Bay, puddles along the canal,
waves back-washing little feet, bird tracks in the sand,
the little moth fluttering at the windowsill,
and blond fields of wheat
as fireplace ashes snap, hornets in the wrong month,
and December's prison arrives, chains and locks us up in blankness.

## The Bottom Of the Well

Here's the empty room. No children's laughter floats down the stairs, in the trash the last IBC cream soda bottle. What good the gem stones in the wooden box, the clothes that suffocate each closet. Dark leather boots deliver December rock salt again. There's no swishing of sleighs in new fallen snow, no pie a la mode for the blues. The well is shallow, nitrate levels test high. Shall I call a dowser to bail me out? No, it's up to me.

# As the Clock Runs Down We Can Still...

blow bubbles with Bazooka Gum, watch children with Fourth of July sparklers, make sandcastle cakes and red, white and blue muffins, amaze at trapeze artists walking on tightropes, allow our dogs to wee on fire hydrants, pretend that superman exists, buy 9 ounces of Johnson's baby powder, smell a neighbor's leaves burning in the fall, hear "American Pie" on the radio, break New Year's resolutions, drink Coke out of cans on the Commons while watching the Labor Day parade, enjoy campfires on Pack Monadnock, drink hot chocolate with whipped cream, hear the train whistle coo, trust that monkey bars will hold, believe diamonds are forever, love the smell of new mown grass, anticipate the aroma of coffee from the unopened Maxwell can, try to make the jigsaw pieces fit, wear pom poms on woolly ski caps, wait for the ruby-throated hummingbird's return, play roadside golf with the kids while cows graze in golden New Hampshire fields, write to Santa at the North Pole, imagine lakes filled with sailboats on hazy summer days, click the lock on the side door at night, turn on an "I love Lucy" lamp.

## But I Do

I thought I'd never see you again but I do when a branch
with five yellow leaves floats to the ground in September, as
a light breeze pushes open my screen door, when Bette Midler
sings "Folks who live on the Hill", when I recall the lamprey
on our brook's edge we squealed as you reeled it in and how we
fished for the rest of the afternoon and only hooked weeds. You're
there in spirit as I sit alone in the porch swing. I remember you when
town workers hook up the iron chains joining the granite posts
to close down Meadowview Cemetery for the winter, attempting
to keep people out. I know we both think *nice try*.

# Gloves

I first wore leather gloves as a child sitting up front in the fourth row pew in the Methodist Episcopal Church on Whalley Avenue in New Haven, Connecticut. It was the thing to do then. Be the proper little lady. But those gloves have disappeared from my life. No more church pews, except at funerals, church concerts or weddings. No longer do I try to reason about God. I just walked out on him. Now I use different kinds of gloves, such as, cotton ones that I can pull weeds with, or latex ones that I can paint my Raleigh Tavern Peach bench with, or ones that I can put on to wash the greasy pots and pans, or wash the walls down with. And with winter gloves and a spade or shovel I can clear away the autumn leaves or toss the snow or dig in the pink chrysanthemums in the spring or build city-wide sand castles at the shore. I just bought a new pair of gloves today. I'll wear them to bed tonight—in my old age to protect against the seasonal ravages. I trust they'll be the key to a semblance of well being as weeks merge into winter—to combat the dryness of the wood stove as the involuntary need to stay indoors to keep the cold winds out of my existence takes over. I'll reside in an embryonic state, go down under, disappear into the thicket of the bed while the down quilt cocoons me until warm air melts the green moss' top hat of snow and crocus blossoms peak through the lawn. Then I'll know I will have made it through another year of storms and cold spells.

## Tea Party

A dazzling welcome from the backseat of your mother's car—little legs kicking up and down and your breathtaking smile. You gather a bouquet of dandelions for our luncheon. Like a mother with cubs, you round up Bunny-Bear, Charlie and Toni in baby carriages and wheel them to your elaborately-set table. Jade, your sea-turtle could not make it and Pierre, your piggy, was upstate. You serve pizza-cake made from wooden blocks, pour apple blossom tea into dainty, pink cups, then sit down next to me. The grass is profoundly greener on my side of the street.

# To My Valentines

    For my grandchildren

You prove angels are on call, make anger disappear. You're my peanut butter cups, my fragile cotton candy. Whether you run across the room to bring me the last grape in the dish or display the principle of gravity with a row boat pump, I know we can truly love another more than we love ourselves. You're the treasures in my life, diamonds with little fingers. I'll forever wipe your tears and hope your lollipop and later dreams in life come true. May you always win at bobbing apples, stretch your minds to the heights of your abilities. You allow me to sing in sync with life as the dusky shadows of age descend. You dress the stars above in satin cloth. I'll never forget your look of gratitude when I found one of your teddy bears lying face-down in the sandbox. You're my vision for the future; you lead me to my inner core of giving. You're life at the front door, a reason for going on, my proof of reincarnation. You're my baby mallards on the pond, you allow me to see beyond the rain. You'll inhabit my heart for as long as snowflakes fall. You, my little mittens, warm and shelter me through it all.

With love,
your grandmother

# Packing

Bunny's rattle, one wooden clog, a sleigh bed I have room for.
In my heart, memories of all these things are intertwined.
Mr. Radio asks, *"Just stuff to pack"*. "No, no, it's much more."

Boxed the brass bed warmer. Snug it is inside the old front door.
I'm taking the mortar and pestle and will not change my mind.
Packed the crystal vase, gone its roses from a nearby shore.

Emily's poems plucked from the top shelf, favorite lines underscored.
Skip gets his mallard decoy; his sweep oar; I've no axe to grind.
Selfish Mr. Radio sings, *"Bring them with you, I implore."*

The cigarette case with safety pins I won't need anymore,
The ladder for changing chandelier bulbs will stay behind.
In the hall, my armless doll presides over all, to be adored,

always a friend for every season, we share a lifelong rapport.
Dad's grandfather clock won't come—its dial can't rewind.
Mr. Radio croons, *"Just stuff you pack?"* "No, no, it is more.

Purple grapes along the trellis, is a memory I'll weep for.
The children's high chairs and rocking horse I never will consign.
I'll gladly abandon the unshielded porch outside the front door.
Mr. Radio sings, *"go south now, my dear, leave it forevermore."*

# Move Back To My Old Hometown

I hang the horseshoe upside down over my new
front door, unstore my rowboat, anchor it down at
the pond. I find the Shaker table slightly scratched
by movers fits perfectly in the front hall once more.
On the way home from the grocery, Susan Blake
invites me to rejoin the Amherst Bridge Club,
my old friend" Scooter" barking "Hello" through
the screen. The house where I raised my kids now
has a badminton net in the front yard, a sparrow pecks
at a cherry fallen from our tree. I rest on Linnea's
granite bench, watch as raindrops plink on the peach
Tavern table, the bird feeder sways in the unnaturally
tropical breeze. I'm ready to call all my grandchildren,
challenge them to checkers, hopscotch, jump rope
when the Admin rings me up to find out
when I'm coming back to work.

## Close Contact

A young couple glides to a Viennese waltz
in their third floor loft "ballroom."
Melodious strands drift down from opened windows,
enchant my 5am walk. In my mind I sway, rise,
then gracefully turn in steps I once knew so well.

## Notes Incarnate...

resound in air when a first dahlia beats through
the soil this dazzling spring day,
in the buzzing of bees heard
outside the green-trimmed screen door in August,
when a neighbor clangs a dinner bell for children
to gather around her laden table,

from cinder blocks with the cadence of beetles
scurrying out after a soaking rain,
in the intonation of a rattle beaten
on the high-chair tray before lunch is served,
in the octave of water as it drips back
into the pond from a lifted canoe paddle,

in the timbre of stacking cords of wood
for cold November eves,
when waves lap against and then draw
back the sand at Long Island Sound,
at the train station when a locomotive bell
clangs kids coming home from college,

in the blues of the wind as it wafts
a woman's silk scarf on an autumn morn,
keyed in the chant of a down blanket
pulled up around shoulders in December,
in our farewell anthem when you finally
have to draw your hand from mine.

# Runaway

Edy's "Cheesecake Diva" was my treat when I was blue,
driving the tractor, waving to the neighbors,
cheeks rosied by sleigh rides down December Hill.
My daughter has the diamond he gave me in the cottage garden.
Gone the bouquets of coral roses,
our strolls along the shoreline of Long Island Sound.
Butterflies have lost some of their grace.
Chopped down the weeping willow, boundary of our field.
Finished, Mozart's concerto I once heard at Carnegie Hall.
Packed away the angel who once looked over our Christmas tree.
Time, you thief, you traitor, you've run out on me.

# Think Of Me. . .

when the train whistle blows at the Yale-New Haven station,
as the pitcher throws a strikeout at Fenway's field of dreams,
when you see Easter eggs tied to trees with lavender strings,
as dandelions invade the lawn and no one's there to dig them up,
after you've shoveled snow and you rest in front of a white birch fire,
when you place gear in the pick-up and sun glints off the silver canoe,
as you pack potato chips and tuna sandwiches
into the straw lunch basket,
when you wash the dishes and leave them to dry,
when church bells toll for weddings and funerals.

## sublime

fill my pine box with down     add soft silky scarves     blow cotton candy around the edges          add maroon     red     yellow leaves put in some hay a dash of mossy grass and     a tall glass of whipped cream     i'll need pot stickers     ibc cream     my toothbrush my car keys     some cash toss in a pair of worn white sneakers     a ping pong ball     one big bar of soap     generously sprinkle  mortons on orvilles *after all     i'm dead*     mix in some ice with sparkling snowflakes but don't get carried away     don't forget marbles from the benton  school playground       throw in a lock of each child's hair     add pink taffy a giant sized dish of my favorite  meringue     puff in a waft of sweet october air        lock it tight       bury it deep

## Where the Grass Is Green

Daisies border the brook where silver trout swim.
Purple onions along the paths.
Muddy garden shoes in the sink.
Box of tangerines on the counter.
It's quiet out on the porch
where we sip ice tea with mint.

## End Of Day

The sun draws ochre darkness across brick buildings along the canal.

Purple ice cream melts in my porcelain dish.

# About the Author

Martha Deborah Hall's poems appear in numerous national journals including, *Bellowing Ark, Common Ground Review, Las Cruces, Old Red Kimono, Tale Spinners, Tapestries, The Poet's Touchstone* and *Watch the Eye*. She is the winner of the 2005 John and Miriam Morris Chapbook contest for her collection *Abandoned Gardens*. Her book *Two Grains in Time* was published by Plain View Press in early 2009. She is a past President of the Amherst Junior Women's Club and was the Amherst Chairman of Alexander Haig's bid for the presidency. Hall holds degrees from Ohio Wesleyan and Columbia University and is currently a real estate broker with Coldwell Banker in Amherst, New Hampshire.

Martha Deborah Hall
Country Mansion Condos, Unit 6
135 Amherst Street
Amherst, NH 03031
603-672-0106
debhall1@myfairpoint.net

www.ingramcontent.com/pod-product-compliance
Lightning Source LLC
Chambersburg PA
CBHW052114070526
44584CB00017B/2473